Presented to

_____

On the occasion of

_____

From

_____

Date

_____

Coffee Talk

A Celebration of
Good Coffee and Great Friends

Ellyn Sanna

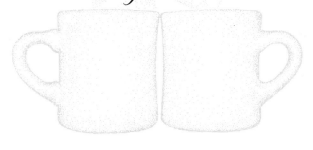

BARBOUR
PUBLISHING, INC.

ecpa Member of the
Evangelical Christian
Publishers Association

Contents

Our world loves coffee. People find drinking a cup of coffee to be a private ritual, a peaceful little space of time that gives their day structure and significance. Even more, coffee is a social ceremony, something we do while we talk with friends. It provides us with moments of relaxation in the midst of our work day.

With caffeine or without, coffee is more than a simple beverage. The very aroma of fresh-ground coffee beans carries with it a whole bundle of feel-good sensations: warmth, comfort, friendship, relaxation, hospitality, intimacy.

A Ceremony of Friendship

Every true friend is a glimpse of God.
—LUCY LARCOM

When friends meet, hearts warm.
—PROVERB

"Come over for a cup of coffee," we say to our friends. What we really mean is, "Let's spend some time together talking." An invitation for coffee is synonymous with an offer of friendship; it means we want to take the time to get to know each other better. In our culture, drinking coffee together has somehow become one of friendship's building blocks, a small and casual ceremony that brings us closer to each other.

Holy Friendship that has medicine for
all the wretchedness is not to be despised.
From God it truly is, that amid the wretchedness of this exile,
we be comforted with the counsel of friends
until we come to Him.
—RICHARD ROLLE (1300-1349)

A friend is a present you give yourself.
—ROBERT LOUIS STEVENSON

Do you know that conversation is one of
the greatest pleasures in life?
—SOMERSET MAUGHAM

When I was first married, we lived in a town several hours from my family and friends. After a long-distance engagement, I had thought that being with my husband every day would be all the companionship I needed—but I found that I was desperately lonely that first year. My husband had lived in the town for several years before our marriage, and he had a busy life already established there—but I had no one to confide in when we argued, no one I knew well enough to call when I was crying, no one with whom I could go clothes shopping, no one with whom I could watch "chick flicks." I loved my husband dearly—but he saw no reason to spend hours talking every day, when in his mind, a well-chosen sentence or two would suffice.

What a relief one day when a woman I met at work asked me to stop over for coffee. We sat on her porch, sipping from steaming mugs, talking about marriage and men, housecleaning and makeup, our mothers and our boss, everything and anything. I came home replete, more in love with my husband than ever after spending some time with another woman.

After that, those coffee talks on her porch became part of our weekly routine, a time we could laugh and analyze our husbands and ourselves to our hearts' content, a time to share and relax.

A person standing alone can be attacked and defeated,
but two can stand back-to-back and conquer.
Three are even better, for a triple-braided cord
is not easily broken.
—ECCLESIASTES 4:12 (NLT)

How it dissolves the barriers that divide us, and loosens all constraint,
and diffuses itself like some fine old cordial through
all the veins of life—this feeling that we understand
and trust each other,
and wish each other heartily well!
—HENRY VAN DYKE

The greatest gift we can give one another is
rapt attention to one another's existence.
—SUE ATCHLEY EBAUGH

What a thing friendship is, world without end!
How it gives the heart and soul a stir-up!
—ROBERT BROWNING

"Women," says my husband, "get up on a Saturday morning and think, 'What am I feeling today?' They devote an hour or two to determining exactly which emotions they are currently entertaining. Then they get together with a friend and spend another two or three hours drinking coffee while they further analyze their feelings, discussing them, comparing and contrasting, and sharing further details of their emotional landscape."

This is obviously a gross exaggeration. But to my mind, the ability to share thoughts helps me not only know my friend better but myself too. The mug is warm between my hands, the rich smell of ground coffee fills my nose with the aroma of comfort and understanding, and our conversation is strung together with slow, thoughtful sips. I come away refreshed, knowing my thoughts are understood, my faults forgiven, and my dreams challenged to step into reality.

I accept that my husband and I approach life from different points of view. That's okay. I love him anyway. But I'll never be convinced that he wouldn't be just a little more self-aware if he had a friend with whom he shared coffee and good talks.

True friends don't spend time gazing into each other's eyes.
They may show great tenderness toward each other,
but they face in the same direction—toward common projects,
interests, goals—above all, toward a common Lord.
—C. S. LEWIS

Friendship renders prosperity more brilliant,
while it lightens adversity by sharing it
and making its burden common.
—CICERO

If you want to improve your understanding, drink coffee.
—SYDNEY SMITH

One of the most beautiful qualities of true friendship is
to understand and to be understood.
—SENECA

In my cupboard are two large creamy green coffee mugs. They exactly match the top half of my kitchen walls. They feel good in my hands. And they are especially dear to me because they were a gift to me from my friend.

All summer, she stops by once a week with fresh-baked muffins, while I have the coffee brewed and ready. While our children play, we talk about work and children, men and housework, our frustrations and God. We laugh until we cry sometimes. Other times we share our hurts and forgive each other's foibles.

Since she's a teacher, our coffee talks end during the school year. But when I take one of those green mugs out of my cupboard, I always think of her and smile, remembering shared laughter.

Two are better than one. . . .
If one person falls,
the other can reach out and help.
But people who are alone when they fall are in real trouble.
—ECCLESIASTES 4:9–10 (NIV, NLT)

To have joy one must share it—
Happiness was born a twin.
—LORD BYRON

I find friendship to be. . .
the true. . .
restorative cordial.
—THOMAS JEFFERSON

Friendships multiply joys and divide griefs.
—H. G. BOHN

A Private Ritual

Go on loving what is good, simple, and ordinary.
—RAINER MARIA RILKE

Coffee is the common man's gold, and like gold,
it brings to every man the feeling of luxury and nobility.
—ABD-AL-KADIR, 1587

Coffee played a big role in our life.
The first thing you did in the morning was put on water,
and the last thing you did at night was take off the pot.
—PAUL PRUDHOMME, quoted by John DeMers,
The Community Kitchen's Complete Guide to Gourmet Coffee

As human beings, we need to impose some sort of structure onto the great chaotic mass of life. Otherwise, we too easily lose our way amid the welter of emotions and events. We use weddings and graduations and funerals for some of the biggest of life's events—but we also have small, private ceremonies that are useful for the ordinary, everyday business. We tend to take these little daily rituals for granted, but our life would be the poorer without them, for these are the moments when we can touch God.

What are these personal ceremonies? I'm sure they're different for each of us. But for me, that morning cup of coffee is somehow essential to the day's progress. Almost mindlessly, I grind the beans, smelling their aroma, and put them in the filter. Then I wait while the coffee maker sighs and drips, and the odor fills the kitchen. At last, I sit down at the table, my cup in hand, looking out at the dogwood tree while I slowly sip the coffee and open my heart to God. By the time I'm done, the kids are pounding down the stairs, and it's time to make breakfast and lunches, braid hair and find matching socks, make sure faces are washed and teeth brushed. But that's okay, because I'm ready now.

That cup of coffee is just a small moment in my life, a quiet little space that somehow opens the day's door, so that I can walk through with a calmer spirit, out into my life's activity.

Sweetening one's coffee is generally
the first stirring event of the day.
—ANONYMOUS

When you pray, go away by yourself. . .
and pray to your Father secretly. Then your Father,
who knows all secrets, will reward you.
—MATTHEW 6:6 (NLT)

Teach us delight in simple things.
—RUDYARD KIPLING

I have measured out my life with coffee spoons.
—T. S. ELIOT, *The Love Song of J. Alfred Prufrock*

When my children take swimming lessons each summer, they swim in the large high school pool, while I watch from the other side of a glass wall. Most of the time the groups of children are too involved with splashing and jumping and paddling to notice the loving audience of parents that watches from behind the wall of windows. But every now and then, each child turns and looks for the one face that matters.

When I see one of my children search for me, I always hold up my hand—my thumb, forefinger, and little finger raised, my two middle fingers down: the "I Love You" sign. My child smiles, and then goes back to swimming, splashing harder, diving straighter, knowing that I'm watching.

God, too, is a loving parent, waiting for a chance to show His children His love. If we don't turn and look for His face, though, we'll miss Him. We need to examine our lives and find those tiny moments where He's studded our lives with "I Love You" signs. All we need to do is look.

When I think of my own life, I see four transition points in my weekdays: first, the moment when I get up and greet the day; then the few minutes after the older two are on the school bus and my youngest is settled in front of "Sesame Street"; next, the quiet ten minutes I take when she leaves for kindergarten—after lunch before I start my own work day; and last of all, the little space when I sit out on my front step waiting for the afternoon school bus, shifting gears back from work to children. I spend each of these four small moments with a cup of decaf in my hand and a prayer in my heart.

These are my "coffee talks" with God. These are the "I Love You" signs I find embedded in my day's routine.

As for me, I look to the LORD. . . .
—MICAH 7:7(NLT)

Very little is needed to make a happy life.
—MARCUS AURELIUS

[Coffee is]. . .*the most precious of blisses.*
—JOHANN SEBASTIAN BACH

Coffee Breaks: Tiny Sabbaths

The Sabbath is a sign of the covenant between me and you forever.
It helps you to remember that I am the LORD, who makes you holy.
Work six days only, but the seventh day must be a day of total rest.
—EXODUS 31:13, 15 (NLT)

Where our work is, there let our joy be.
—TERTULLIAN, C. 220

The Hebrew word *sabbath* means simply "rest." When God made us, He knew we would need to rest from our work; and apparently He also knew how hard that would be for some of us, for He made the sabbath not merely a suggestion, but a commandment. Sabbath times are not to be refused because we're too busy; instead, we should "make every effort to enter that rest" (Heb. 4:11, NIV). These are times when we separate ourselves from the business of life so that we can be refreshed and renewed.

For many of us, we find a little sabbath in the midst of each work day: our coffee break. This is the moment in our busy schedule when we can pause and relax. Over a hot cup of coffee, we laugh with friends and momentarily draw away from the day's pressures. Or we sit alone at our desk, drinking in peace and a renewed sense of perspective alone with our coffee.

Either way, this is a moment we can offer to God. Historically, God's people have connected sabbath times with worship, for when we take time from our work, we clear our minds so that we can think consciously about God.

Research shows that people work quicker and more efficiently if they're give regular coffee breaks. Savor the full gift of these small sabbaths.

Coffee detracts nothing from your intellect; on the contrary,
your stomach is freed by it and no longer distresses your brain;
it will not hamper your mind with troubles
but give freedom to its working.
Suave molecules of Mocha stir up your blood, without causing excessive
heat; the organ of thought receives from it a feeling of sympathy;
work becomes easier and you sit down without distress.
—PRINCE TALLEYRAND (1754-1838)

The Aroma of Love

If I were a woman, I'd wear coffee as a perfume.
—JOHN VAN DRUTEN

Where coffee is served there is grace and splendor.
—ANONYMOUS

To a coffee lover, nothing smells so good as fresh coffee beans. My sister has a friend who loves the aroma so much that each time she opens a new can of coffee, she holds it out to her children and commands them to breathe deeply. "Whenever you smell this in life," she says, "think of me." She can think of no better thing to which to tie her memory, and she hopes that when her children are old and she is long dead, that rich, dark smell will speak to them of the same love and acceptance that she offered them.

Keep on loving each other. . . .
Do not forget to entertain strangers,
for by so doing some people have
entertained angels without knowing it.
—HEBREWS 13:1-2 (NIV)

The first time I drank coffee was when I was in high school. The guidance counselor and his secretary kept a pot hot for any students who wandered into their office. I remember how welcoming the smell was, how much it spoke to me of maturity and comfort. High school wasn't always a very easy world; I didn't quite fit the mold that would have made me accepted and popular, and adolescent anguish is particularly painful. But in the guidance office, breathing that warm, dark brown aroma while I sipped the grown-up brew, I caught a glimpse of a world where I'd fit, a world of ideas and words and laughter.

You are as welcome as flowers in May.
—WILLIAM SHAKESPEARE

I had a perfect honeymoon. Sometimes reality falls short of our fantasies, but not this time. We walked the cobblestone streets of Quebec City hand in hand, poking our heads into quaint little shops, eating in cozy, European restaurants while we looked into each other's eyes. My husband practiced his French while we bought each other gifts—a leather briefcase I still carry, a carved head of a proud African woman that stands on our bookcase now. And every morning we'd drink *café au lait,* strong and sweet, with our croissants.

Fourteen years and three kids later, my husband and I don't have much time in our day for looking into each other's eyes. Mornings, I'm already at my desk working while he hurries to get dressed and out the door. We pass each other in the kitchen usually, where we grab a quick kiss while I make us each a cup of *café au lait.*

But to my mind, the coffee's even stronger and sweeter than it was in Quebec City.

> *Good coffee is black as sin,*
> *pure as the angels,*
> *strong as death,*
> *and sweet as love.*
> —CREOLE SAYING

Some days at mealtime, all I hear is a chorus of "Can I have a drink?" "Can you cut my meat?" "I want juice!" "You forgot to give me a fork!" "Mom, Micaela spilled her milk on my bread." I jump up and down like a jack-in-the-box. Rarely do I get to sit and relax over a meal. And sometimes, I can't help but resent feeling like the family waitress—especially since none of them ever leave a tip.

So when I escaped last Saturday to our local diner to meet a friend for breakfast, how good it felt to have someone wait on me for a change. "Here you go," said our favorite waitress, putting a cup of steaming decaf in front of me before I'd even asked. With no prompting from me, she gave me the two creams I always put in my coffee. "I'm glad you got to run away this morning," she whispered in my ear.

I took a slow hot sip with tears in my eyes. Sometimes, I realized, God hands out His love in coffee cups.

There is no beverage which is held
in more universal esteem
than good coffee.
—Eliza Acton, 1845

A History of Hospitality, Good Conversation, and Prayer

Share with God's people. . . .
Practice hospitality.
—ROMANS 12:13 (NIV)

With modern society in the throes of a love affair with coffee, historians have tried to tie coffee to the writings of the ancient world. After all, how could ancient people have survived without coffee? The very idea is hard to imagine.

That's why some have claimed that Homer mentions coffee; they insist that the *nepenthe* that Helen of Troy brought with her from Egypt, sort of her hostess gift, must have actually been our favorite brew. Others say that the Lacedaemonians' "black broth," a part of their traditional hospitality, was obviously coffee. And then of course, we'd all like to find coffee in the Bible; surely David must have written a psalm about it *somewhere*. Or what about the red pottage for which Esau sold his birthright? Who would do that for a bowl of lentils, after all? But for a cup of coffee? Well, that we can understand. Or how about the parched grain that Boaz ordered for Ruth? Makes sense, doesn't it, that he was doing what we all do when we're feeling hospitable—offering his guest a nice hot cup of coffee? And remember when Abigail gave David five measures of parched corn, hoping to appease his wrath? Well, obviously the translators used the word *corn* loosely, because what the original author must have meant is probably five hospitable canisters of roasted coffee beans. Right?

Actually, however, coffee originated in the Arab world. One legend says that a goat herder named Kaldi, who lived in upper Egypt or Abyssinia, noticed that his goats were more lively after crunching on a particular kind of cherry. After watching his goats "abandoning themselves to the most extravagant prancing," Kaldi decided he might as well try the fruit himself. Soon after, a monk from the nearby monastery was surprised to see Kaldi and his goats leaping and prancing with unusual energy. The monks experimented with boiling the cherries—and to their surprise, they found that the dark drink helped them pray better. Instead of falling asleep over their evening devotions, they came to God with refreshed alertness. Coffee had been discovered.

The Turks have a drink of black colour. . . .
They swallow it hot as it comes from the fire
and they drink it in long draughts, not at dinner time,
but as a kind of dainty and sipped slowly
while talking with one's friends.
One cannot find any meetings among them
where they drink it not. . . .
—ITALIAN EXPLORER, 1615

The Arabs and Egyptians make a sort of decoction of it,
which they drink instead of wine:
and it is sold in all their public houses. . . .
—PROSPERO ALPINI, 1580

As European explorers ventured into the Arab world in the sixteenth century, they encountered coffee for the first time. They were so taken with the new beverage that they were certain it must have medicinal properties. By the seventeenth century, they had brought it with them back to their own countries and coffee houses spread throughout Europe. As European countries colonized the West Indies and South America, they discovered that coffee could be grown there quite profitably.

Closes the Orifice of the Stomack, fortifies the Heat within,
helpeth Digestion, quickneth the Spirits, makes the Heart lightsom,
is good against Eye-sores, Coughs, or Colds, Rhumes,
Consumptions, Head-ach, Dropsie, Gout, Scurvy. . .
and many others.
—PUBLICK ADVISER, 1657

This Rare Arabian cordial Use,
then thou mayst all the Doctors' shops refuse.
—ADVERTISEMENT FROM 1674

Choicest Mocha coffee [served] *in*
tiny cups of egg-shell porcelain,
hot, strong, and fragrant,
poured out in saucers of gold and silver. . .
to the grand dames, who fluttered their fans
with many grimaces, bending their piquant faces. . .
over the new and steaming beverage.
—ISAAC D'ISRAELI, *Curiosities of Literature*

During the Enlightenment, coffee houses became the spiritual and intellectual centers for new thoughts about democracy and human equality. These coffee houses became known as penny universities, for anyone craving intellectual stimulation could pay for it with the cost of a cup of coffee—one penny.

In the New World, Daniel Webster called a Boston coffee house, the Green Dragon, the "headquarters of the Revolution." Early English settlers may have preferred tea, but with one fell swoop, the Boston Tea Party in 1773 created a country of coffee drinkers.

*Hot, black and
strong enough to walk by itself.*
—19th-century coffee preference,
JOEL, DAVID, & KARL SCHAPIRA,
The Book of Coffee and Tea

Mass consumption of coffee began in the 1800s. The stimulating beverage had found itself a permanent home in the workplaces created by the Industrial Revolution. It helped workers get through their grueling sixteen-hour work days, and it kept them awake long enough at home to interact with their families. Coffee was a fixture in most everyone's life.

Today, coffee grows throughout the world in tropical and subtropical regions. The trees require a constant temperature and sixty to eighty inches of annual rain.

Coffee plants are actually an evergreen shrub. They produce jasmine-scented white blossoms that mature into red cherries. The coffee bean is the fruit's seed; two beans grow face-to-face within each cherry. Each tree produces only a pound to a pound and a half of roasted coffee each year—about four thousand hand-picked beans.

Arabica and robusta are the two different species of coffee

trees. Arabica grows in the mountains, and it is the coffee used for today's popular specialty coffees. Robusta grows at lower altitudes. It has twice the caffeine content as arabica, and it is used for instant and commercial coffees.

CAFFEINE OR DECAF?

Caffeine is a mild stimulant that's found in coffee, tea, chocolate, cola, and headache medicine. Tolerance to caffeine varies from person to person, but for most of us, caffeine acts merely as a gentle aid to thought, productivity, and conversation.

Decaffeinated coffee is created by removing the caffeine from the green coffee beans. One method uses a solvent to pull the caffeine out of the beans while leaving the flavors intact. The solvent vaporizes when the beans are then roasted. Another method, the Swiss Water Process, submerges the beans in very hot water and then percolates the water through activated charcoal. The beans are then returned to the water to reabsorb the flavorful oils. This method is slightly more expensive.

Coffee Roast

LIGHT ROAST:
> *cinnamon-colored, sour tasting. Most commercial canned coffee is light roasted.*

MEDIUM ROAST:
> *chestnut-colored, full range of flavors. Used for specialty coffees.*

DARK ROAST:
> *the color of bittersweet chocolate, oily, with a smoky and bitter taste. Used for Espresso and Italian coffees.*

VERY DARK ROAST:
> *black, oily, bitter. Used in French coffees.*

Recipes

Old-Fashioned Coffee Soda

3 cups chilled double-strength
    soda
1 tablespoon sugar
1 cup half-and-half

4 scoops (1 pint) coffee
    ice cream
¾ cup chilled club soda
whipped cream for garnish

Combine the coffee and sugar. Blend in the half-and-half. Fill four tall glasses halfway with the coffee mixture. Add a scoop of ice cream to each glass. Fill to the top with soda. Add a dollop of whipped cream to each glass.

COFFEE TIP

Too fine a grind causes a bitter brew, because the beans have more surface area where they can be exposed to the water. Too coarse a grind results in watery coffee, because the water runs through the coffee too quickly.

Coffee Chili

1 cup dried red beans
2 tbsps vegetable oil
3 cloves minced garlic
1 ½ tbsps chili powder
1 tsp dried thyme
1 tsp pepper
1 cup beef broth
salt to taste
cream for garnish
cilantro sprigs

1 cup extra-strength coffee
½ cup chopped onion
2 lbs sirloin steak, chopped
   into ½-inch cubes
1 tsp dried oregano
1 tsp cumin
1 can (14 ½ oz) tomato
   puree or crushed sour
   tomatoes
grated Monterey Jack cheese
   for garnish

Cover the beans with ¾ cup coffee and soak overnight.

In a deep casserole or pot, heat 1 tbsp oil and sauté the onion and garlic over medium heat until soft (about 10 minutes). Set them aside and add to remaining oil to brown the steak cubes.

Add the remaining ¼ cup coffee, spices, and tomatoes. Bring to a boil, stir, and allow to simmer for 10 minutes. Add the beef broth and the drained beans and bring to a boil over medium heat. Reduce heat and simmer for 1 hour. Season with salt.

Serve in individual bowls and top with sour cream, cheese, and cilantro sprigs.

Meat Loaf

1 ½ lbs ground beef
½ lb ground pork
¾ cup plus 2 tbsps cold coffee
1 tbsp mustard
1 tsp salt

1 lb ground veal
1 ½ cup soft bread crumbs
1 egg, slightly beaten
1 tbsp Worcestershire sauce

Pack the mixture into a loaf pan and bake for 45 to 50 minutes in a 350-degree oven.

COFFEE TIP

Use 2 level tablespoons of coffee for 6 ounces of water. (Six ounces will fill a normal cup, but not a large mug.) If you like your coffee strong, use more grounds, but don't use less coffee if you like your coffee weaker. Instead, dilute your brew with hot water. Otherwise, you will over-extract the beans, making a bitter beverage.

> *Looks can be deceiving—*
> *it's eating that's believing.*
> —JAMES THURBER

Coffee Pecan Pie

COMBINE:

3 eggs

¼ cup molasses

½ cup double strength coffee

¼ tsp salt

¾ cup light corn syrup

2 tbsps melted butter

1 tsp vanilla

ADD:

1 cup chopped pecans

4 tbsps flour

Pour ingredients into an unbaked pie shell. Bake 40 to 45 minutes at 375 degrees, or until firm. Garnish with whipped cream.

Coffee is the crowning of a grand dinner. . .
the piéce de rèsistance. . . .
—LAFCADIO HEARN, *La Cuisine Creolee,*
19th-century cookbook

Coffee Cake

2 cups flour

½ tsp baking soda

¼ tsp allspice

¼ tsp nutmeg

½ cup chopped walnuts or pecans

¼ cup brown sugar

3 eggs

1 tsp baking powder

dash of salt

¼ tsp ground cloves

¼ tsp ginger

½ cup butter

½ cup honey

½ cup coffee

Bake in a 9-inch square pan at 350 degrees for 35-45 minutes. Dust with confectioners' sugar.

COFFEE TIP

Air and moisture quickly steal coffee's flavorful oils. To keep the coffee's flavor, buy and store whole beans; grind them only when you're ready to use them immediately. Store beans in an airtight container in the freezer.

Chocolate Swirl Coffee Cake

STIR TOGETHER:

$^1/_3$ cup flaked coconut

$^1/_4$ cup sugar

$^1/_3$ cup chopped nuts

1 tbsp melted butter or margarine

Set aside.

MIX:

2 cups Bisquick

1 egg

2 tbsps melted butter or margarine

$^1/_4$ cup sugar

$^3/_4$ cup milk

Pour into 8 x 8-inch square pan. Spoon $^1/_3$ cup melted chocolate chips over batter and cut with a knife several times to make a marbled effect. Sprinkle coconut mixture evenly over the top. Bake 20 to 25 minutes in a 400-degree oven.

Eat, O friends, and drink;
drink your fill.
—SONG OF SOLOMON 5:1 (NIV)

For the happy heart,
life is a continual feast.
—PROVERBS 15:15 (NLT)

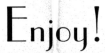

Enjoy!